PAINT BY NUMBERS
DOGS FOR KIDS

AGES 4-8

Paint By Number Coloring Book for Kids

1= blue 2= brown 3=yellow 4=red 5=white 6=black 7=pink

1 yellow

2 vivid yellow

3 **4** **5** **6** **7**

1 = green   4 = yellow
2 = red   5 = brown
3 = tan   6 = pink

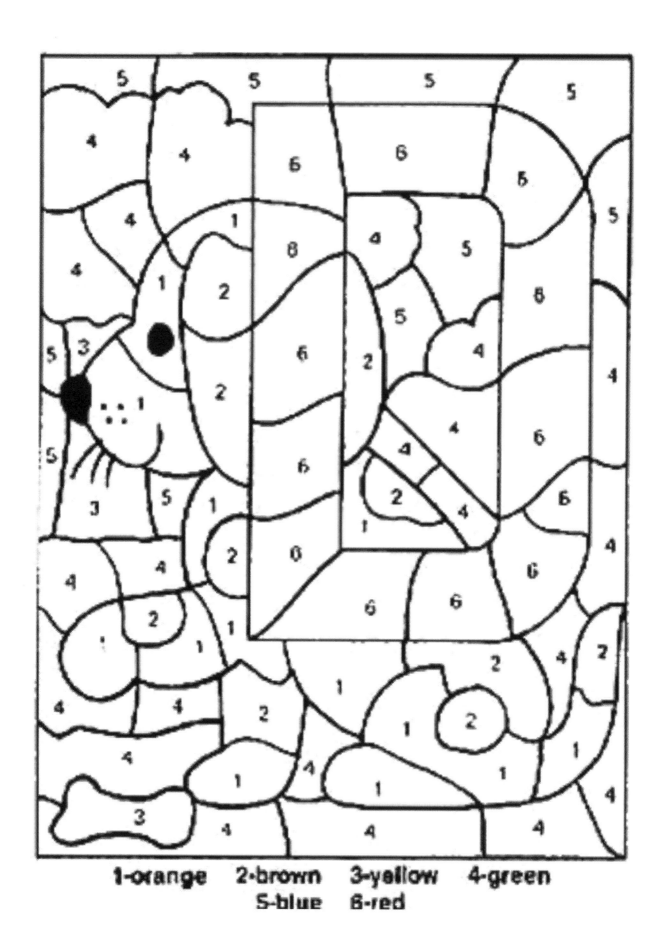

1-orange   2-brown   3-yellow   4-green
5-blue   6-red

black	= 1	pink	= 4	green	= 7
brown	= 2	white	= 5		
tan	= 3	dark brown	= 6		

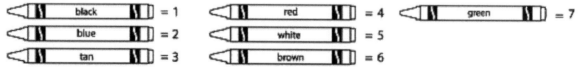

black = 1   red = 4   green = 7

blue = 2   white = 5

tan = 3   brown = 6

1. blue 2.yellow 3.brown
6.green 7.grey 8.beige 9.pink 10.red

black	= 1	blue	= 4
dark brown	= 2	white	= 5
tan	= 3	brown	= 6

1 - black   2 - brown   3 - yellow   4 - purple

5 - red   6 - green   7 - orange   8 - blue

black	= 1	red	= 4	gray	= 7
pink	= 2	white	= 5	green	= 8
tan	= 3	brown	= 6	blue	= 9

1 = red   3 = blue   5 = brown   7 = orange

2 = yellow   4 = green   6 = black

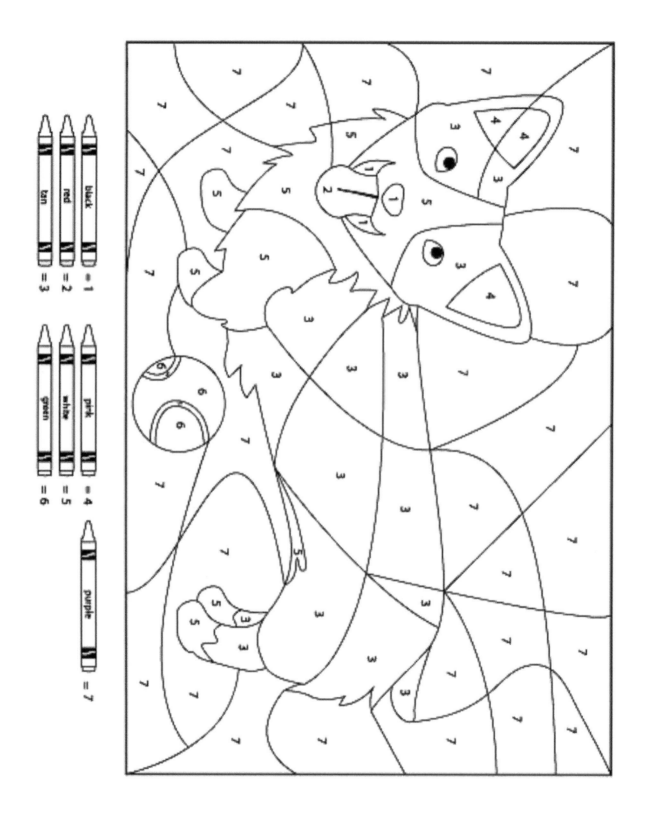

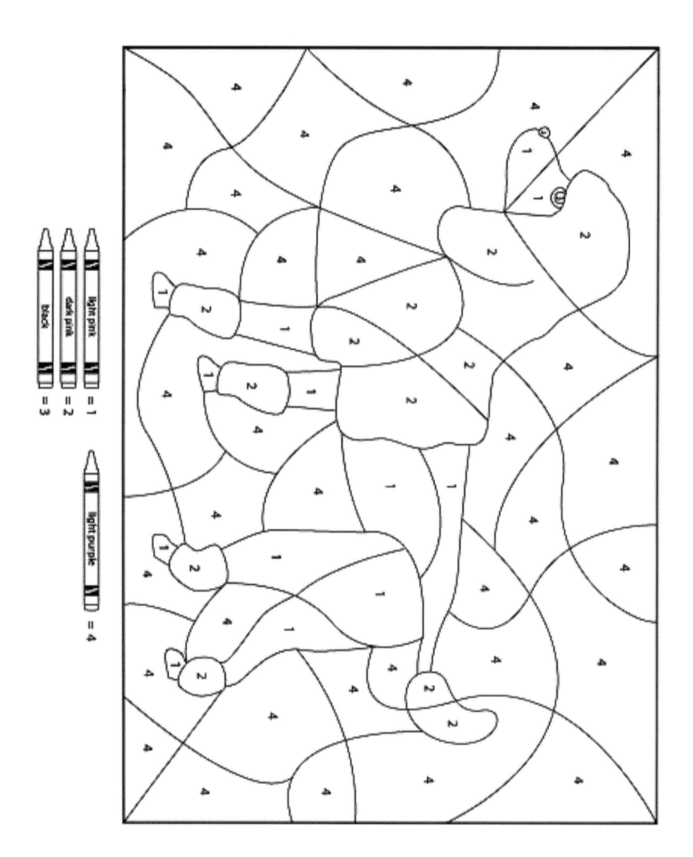

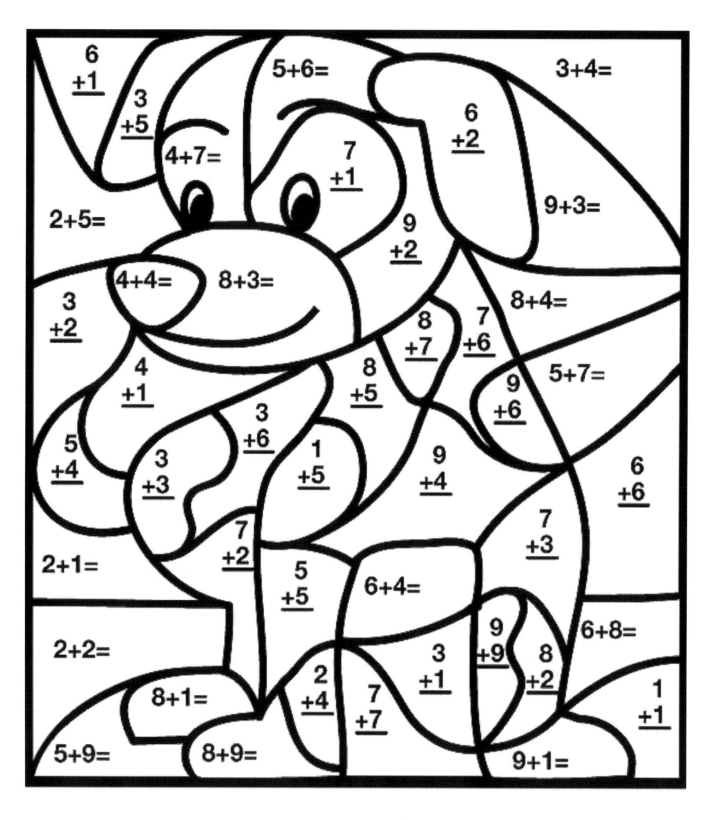

| Brown | 9, 10, 11, 13, 17 | Green | 2, 4, 14 |
| Black | 6, 8, 15, 18 | Sky Blue | 3, 5, 7, 12 |

1-Orange 2-Brown 3-Red 4-Yellow 5-Green 6-Pink 7-Blue

1 - white   2 - light blue   3 - green   4 - dark green
5 - beige   6 - orange   7 - brown   8 - gray

1. Green   2. Grey   3. Red   4. Blue   5. Brown

Color Key

1 BROWN

2 YELLOW

3 BLACK

4 RED

5 ORANGE

6 PURPLE

7 PINK

8 GREEN

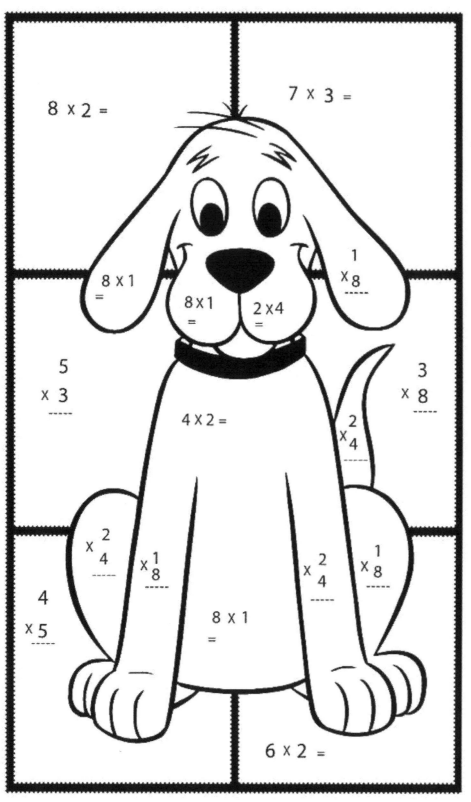

8 x 2 =

7 X 3 =

8 X 1

1
x 8
-----

8 x 1
=

8 X 1
=

2 x 4
=

5
x 3

3
x 8
-----

4 X 2 =

2
x 4

2
x 4
-----

x 1
8

4
x 5

2
x 4
-----

x 1
8
-----

8 X 1
=

6 X 2 =

8 =**Yellow**

16 = **Green**

21 = **Red**

24 = **Blue**

12 = **Green**

20 = **Pink**

15 = **Brown**

1 Blue   2 Green   3 Brown   4 Yellow   5 Grey   6 Purple
7 White

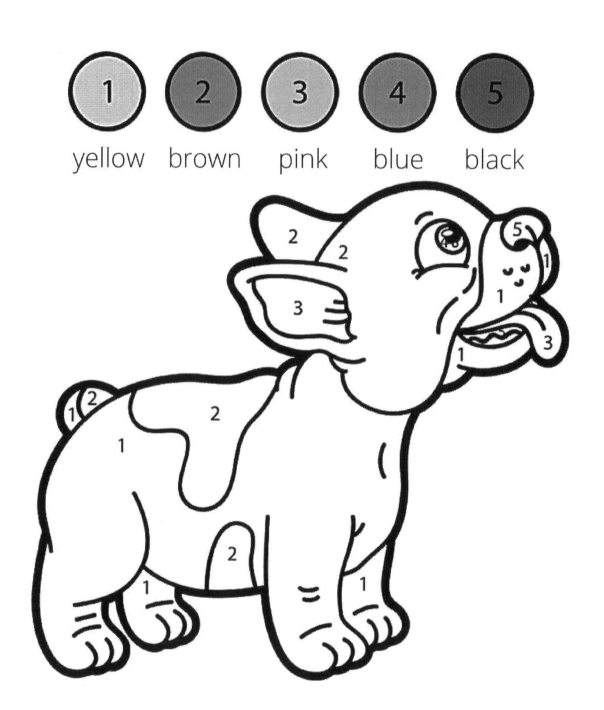

black = 1	blue = 4	
dark brown = 2	white = 5	
tan = 3	brown = 6	

1 = blue   5 = brown
2 = gray   6 = cream
3 = green   7 = peach
4 = yellow

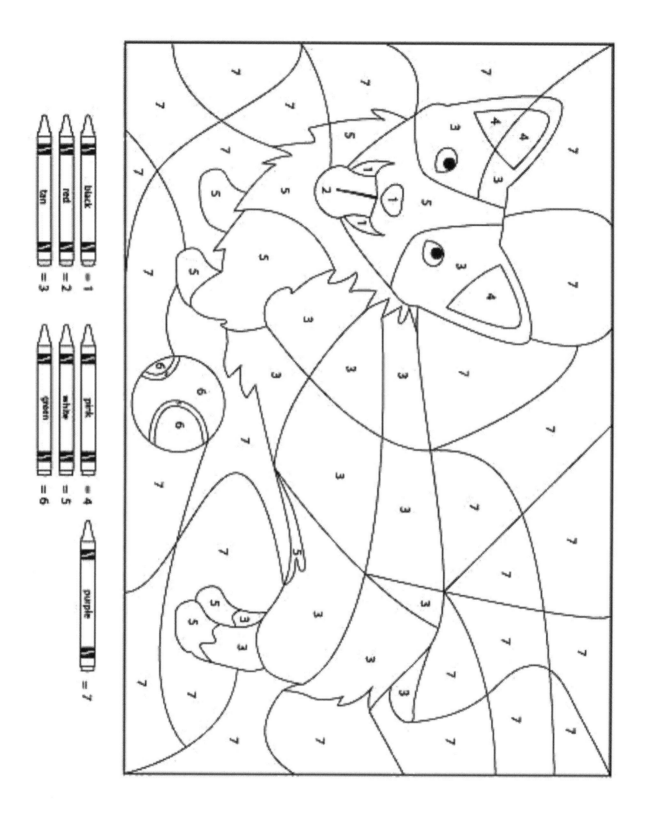

1.redish-brown, 2.orangeish-brown, 3.yellowish-brown, 4.blue, 5.gold

6.black
7.white
8.grey
9.green

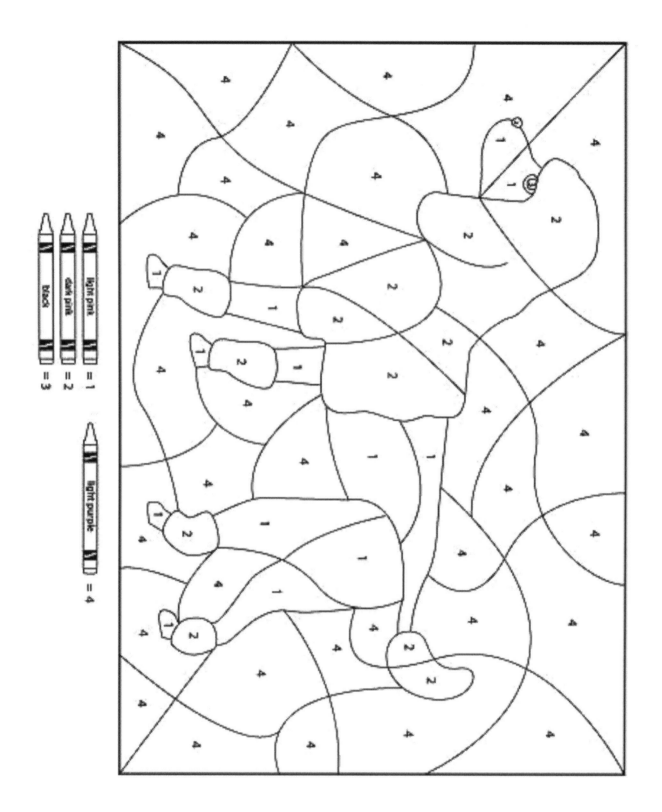

1. White   4. Purple   7. Red   10. Orange
2. Brown   5. Sky blue   8. Olive green
3. Pink   6. Yellow   9. Green

1 - black   **2 - brown**   **3 - yellow**   **4 - purple**

5 - red   **6 - green**   **7 - orange**   **8 - blue**

1 - light blue 2 - dark green 3 - green 4 - yellow
5 - orange 6 - beige 7 - brown 8 - red

COLOR BY NUMBER

1. Red	4. Blue	7. Purple
2. Yellow	5. Orange	8. Pink
3. Green	6. Brown	9. Grey

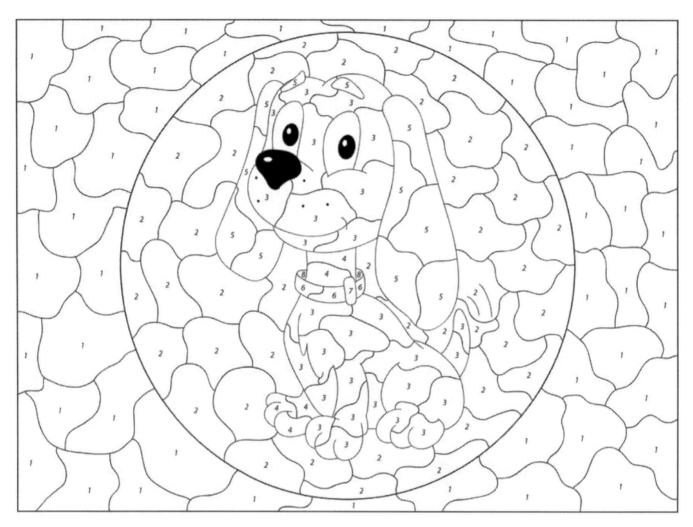

 blue green 3 brown 4 dark brown

5 black 6 red 7 yellow 8 orange

1= brown   3= blue   5= red
2= yellow   4= green   6= pink

Made in the USA
Las Vegas, NV
28 February 2022

44712130R20042